THE MINDSET OF MONEY

" UNLOCKING THE MONEY MYSTERY FOR FINANCIAL ACHIEVEMENT"

BY

TONY D. LAMON

TABLE OF CONTENTS

Introduction

In the intricate tapestry of personal finance, where dreams of prosperity and financial security interweave with the stark realities of budgeting, investments, and economic dynamics, there exists a pervasive force often underestimated—the power of mindset. Welcome to "The Mindset of Money: Unlocking the Money Mystery for Financial Achievement," a transformative exploration into the realms where psychology meets finance, where beliefs shape destinies, and where the mystery of money is unraveled.

The financial landscape, as vast and diverse as the aspirations it holds, serves as the backdrop to our journey. In this introduction, we set the stage for an odyssey through the intricacies of personal finance, inviting readers to embark on a voyage that transcends traditional financial guides.

Imagine the financial landscape as an uncharted terrain, filled with opportunities and challenges. The first steps into this realm are not just steps but a prelude to a journey—one that promises not only financial wisdom but a profound understanding of the role mindset plays in sculpting our financial destinies.

At the heart of our exploration lies a fundamental truth: the mindset we adopt toward money is a silent force, an invisible hand that guides our financial decisions and shapes the outcomes of our endeavors. Delving into this truth, we unveil the profound impact of beliefs, attitudes, and mental frameworks on financial success. This exploration becomes a foundational pillar, emphasizing the transformative potential inherent in cultivating a positive money mindset.

As we venture deeper, we confront the enigma of money itself—the "Money Mystery." Picture it as a puzzle, a complex amalgamation of psychological, societal, and personal factors contributing to the elusive nature of financial success. This book seeks to decode this mystery, offering readers a unique perspective on the intricate dance between mindset and money. It's not just about the dollars and cents; it's about understanding the intricate interplay that shapes our financial reality. What sets "The Mindset of Money" apart is its holistic approach. Beyond the conventional advice of saving, investing, and budgeting, this book extends an invitation to explore the often-overlooked dimension of mindset. It's an invitation to challenge preconceived notions and embrace transformative perspectives. In doing so, we aim not just to accumulate wealth but to cultivate a sustainable and empowering relationship with money.

"The Essence of 'The Mindset of Money'" section serves as a manifesto, declaring the book's purpose—to redefine the essence of financial success. It underscores the profound impact of adopting a positive money mindset, laying the groundwork for real-world transformations that await those who immerse themselves in its principles. This is not just a book about wealth accumulation; it's about creating a paradigm shift, redefining the very essence of our relationship with money.

As readers turn the pages that follow, they are not merely engaging with a book; they are embarking on an interactive guide—an odyssey towards financial enlightenment. Whether one seeks stability, wealth creation, or a breakthrough from financial challenges, the journey unfolds within these pages. "The Mindset of Money" is not a static collection of information; it is a dynamic roadmap, a companion on the journey

to transform financial
reality.

Welcome to a journey
where mindset meets
money, where financial
achievement is not just a
destination but a
transformative experience.
The odyssey begins now,
and within these pages, the
mysteries surrounding
financial success are
unveiled, one insightful
revelation at a time.

Chapter 1

Navigating the Financial Landscape: A Prelude to Transformation.

Imagine standing at the
edge of a vast financial
landscape, a panorama that

extends beyond the horizon, filled with aspirations, challenges, and opportunities. This introduction serves as a prelude to our transformative journey, offering a glimpse into the diverse terrains we are about to explore. The financial landscape, much like a rich tapestry, is woven with threads of personal goals, societal expectations, and economic forces. It is a canvas upon which individuals paint their dreams, chart their courses, and confront the realities of fiscal responsibility.

As we take those initial steps into this uncharted territory, it is essential to recognize that this is not a mere journey through spreadsheets and bank statements; rather, it is a profound exploration of the human relationship with money. The financial landscape is not static; it evolves with the ebb and flow of economic tides, shaping the financial destinies of individuals and communities alike. In this dynamic environment, understanding the nuances of personal finance becomes a crucial skill, akin to navigating uncharted waters.

This prelude invites readers to reflect on their own position within this expansive financial panorama. What are the towering peaks of their financial aspirations? What valleys of challenges lie ahead? The journey we embark upon is not just a guide through the labyrinth of financial principles; it is an opportunity for self-discovery and transformation. By acknowledging the vastness of the financial landscape, readers are encouraged to embrace the complexities that come with it, viewing challenges not as obstacles but as stepping stones to financial growth.

Consider this section as the opening notes of a symphony, setting the tone for the chapters that follow. It's an acknowledgment that each reader brings a unique melody to the orchestra of personal finance, and through understanding the lay of the financial land, one can better compose the harmonies of their financial journey.

1.2 The Silent Force: Mindset in Financial Success.

In the vast expanse of personal finance, where numbers meet aspirations and decisions shape destinies, the significance of mindset emerges as a silent force—an invisible hand that guides the trajectory of our financial journeys. This section delves into the profound impact of beliefs, attitudes, and mental frameworks on financial success, positioning mindset not merely as a companion on the journey but as the very compass that navigates the intricate paths of fiscal prosperity.

Consider for a moment the decisions you make about

money—the choices, the trade-offs, the investments, and the savings. These actions are not solely dictated by financial knowledge; they are profoundly influenced by the lens through which you view money. The beliefs you hold about wealth, success, and your own financial worth serve as the foundational elements of your financial mindset. This introduction invites readers to acknowledge the potency of this silent force, urging them to reflect on the unconscious beliefs that shape their financial behaviors.

Financial success is not merely about accumulating wealth; it's about fostering a mindset that aligns with prosperity. By recognizing the role of mindset, readers are empowered to embark on a transformative journey—one that transcends traditional financial advice and taps into the core of their beliefs. The pages that follow are not just repositories of information; they are mirrors reflecting the relationship between mindset and financial outcomes.

To understand the power of mindset, consider two individuals facing similar financial challenges. One, armed with a positive and resilient mindset, sees setbacks as opportunities for growth, adapting strategies to overcome obstacles. The other, burdened by a negative mindset, might view the same challenges as insurmountable, leading to stagnation or even financial decline. This section is a call to awareness, urging readers to recognize that financial decisions are not isolated events but manifestations of deep-seated beliefs.

As we explore the silent force of mindset, it becomes apparent that it is both a product and a shaper of our financial experiences. Our beliefs about money are often inherited from familial, societal, and cultural influences. Yet, this introduction emphasizes that mindset is not fixed; it is malleable and subject to change. By understanding the roots of one's financial mindset, readers can actively cultivate a positive perspective, fostering an environment where financial success becomes not just a goal but a natural outcome.

1.3 Decoding the Money Mystery

As we step further into the realm of personal finance, we encounter the enigmatic "Money Mystery"—a complex interplay of psychological, societal, and personal factors contributing to the elusive nature of financial success. Picture this mystery as a puzzle waiting to be solved, each piece representing a facet of our relationship with money. This section serves as the guide to decoding this mystery, encouraging readers to explore the layers that veil the true essence of financial achievement.

Consider the intricacies involved in making financial decisions. Why do certain choices feel intuitive, while others create uncertainty? The Money Mystery acknowledges that these decisions are not solely rational; they are influenced by emotions, societal expectations, and deeply ingrained beliefs. This introduction invites readers to engage in a process of unraveling, to question the assumptions they hold about money, and to recognize the external forces shaping their financial perspectives. Unveiling the Money Mystery involves navigating through the societal narratives that often define success and wealth. It prompts readers to critically examine the cultural influences, societal norms, and preconceived notions that may be steering their financial ship. By peeling back the layers of this mystery, readers gain a deeper understanding of the forces at play, empowering them to make conscious and informed financial choices. This section is an invitation to embrace the complexity of the Money Mystery rather than shy away from it. It emphasizes that decoding this mystery is not a one-size-fits-all endeavor; each individual's journey is unique. Through exploration and introspection, readers can begin to decipher their own relationship with money, transforming the mystery into a source of empowerment and self-awareness.

1.4 The Essence of "The Mindset of Money"

With the landscape defined, the mindset acknowledged, and the Money Mystery introduced, we delve into the essence of "The Mindset of Money." This section articulates the book's purpose—to redefine the very essence of financial success. It emphasizes that this book is not merely a compilation of financial principles; it is a guide to cultivate a mindset that transcends conventional notions of wealth.

Consider this essence as the heartbeat of the book, pulsating with the idea that financial success is not solely measured in monetary terms. It's about fostering a mindset that appreciates the holistic nature of prosperity—one that integrates financial well-being with personal fulfillment, purpose, and a sense of abundance. The essence underscores that true financial achievement is not just about amassing wealth; it is about creating a life that aligns with one's values and aspirations.

1.5 Embarking on Your Financial Odyssey.

As we conclude the introduction, readers are invited to see the journey that lies ahead not as a static accumulation of information but as a dynamic odyssey. This section serves as a call to action, urging readers to actively engage in their financial transformation. The financial odyssey embarked upon is more than a linear progression; it's a continuous loop of learning, reflection, and growth.

Consider this invitation as the crossing of a threshold, signaling the beginning of a transformative adventure. It emphasizes that "The Mindset of Money" is not a passive read but an active participation in shaping one's financial destiny. Whether the goal is stability, wealth creation, or overcoming financial challenges, this section encourages readers to embrace the journey with an open mind, ready to challenge assumptions, explore new perspectives, and enact positive changes in their financial lives....

Chapter 2

Understanding Money Mindset: The Psychological Blueprint of Financial Behavior.

Understanding money mindset is delving into the intricate tapestry of beliefs, attitudes, and perceptions that shape our relationship with wealth. It is the acknowledgment that our financial decisions are not merely driven by rational calculations but are deeply rooted in the subconscious currents of our minds. This exploration involves recognizing the lens through which we view money—a lens forged by personal experiences, cultural influences, and societal expectations. Money mindset is a dynamic force, evolving with each financial encounter. It encompasses our thoughts on abundance, scarcity, success, and even failure. To comprehend money mindset is to navigate the behavioral nuances outlined by cognitive biases, understanding how these mental shortcuts influence our financial behaviors. It is a journey that encourages introspection, prompting us to question and, if necessary, reshape our deeply ingrained beliefs about wealth. Moreover, understanding money mindset extends beyond individual reflections; it involves challenging prevailing myths and misconceptions that may be hindering financial empowerment. It is a quest for financial self-awareness, empowering individuals to make informed decisions that align with their long-term goals. In essence, grasping the intricacies of the money mindset is an ongoing process of self-discovery and enlightenment, laying the foundation for a more intentional and empowered approach to personal finance..

2.1 Defining Money Mindset: The Lens Through Which We View Wealth

At its core, defining money mindset is an exploration into the deeply ingrained perspectives, beliefs, and attitudes that individuals hold regarding wealth. It serves as a compass, shaping the way individuals perceive and engage with financial matters. This lens through which we view wealth is not a static or uniform entity but a dynamic mental landscape, molded by a myriad of factors. Consider this lens as a filter through which financial decisions are processed. It encompasses our beliefs about abundance or scarcity, our attitudes toward success and failure, and our overall emotional connection to money. Defining money mindset invites individuals to peel back the layers of their financial beliefs, encouraging an introspective journey into the influences that have shaped these perspectives. This section prompts readers to reflect on their own financial narratives, considering the impact of early experiences, familial influences, and societal expectations. The lens of money mindset is not a monolithic entity but a spectrum of perspectives, acknowledging the diversity in individuals' approaches to wealth. By defining money mindset in

this nuanced way, readers
are empowered to
recognize the fluidity and
complexity of their own
financial beliefs, laying the
groundwork for a more
intentional and informed
relationship with money.

2.2 The Impact of Beliefs on Financial Behavior: Navigating the Behavioral Economics of Finance

Moving beyond the
definition, this section
delves into the profound
impact of beliefs on
financial behavior, drawing
insights from the realm of
behavioral economics.
Behavioral economics
illuminates the intricate
ways in which cognitive

biases and heuristics shape our decision-making processes in the financial arena.

Here, readers navigate the fascinating terrain of psychological tendencies such as loss aversion, mental accounting, and the endowment effect. Loss aversion, for instance, elucidates why individuals tend to feel the pain of financial losses more acutely than the pleasure of equivalent gains. Understanding these biases is akin to holding a mirror to our own decision-making, revealing the subtle influences that may sway us toward irrational financial choices....

2.3 Unpacking Money Myths and

Misconceptions: Challenging Assumptions for Financial Empowerment

This section invites readers to embark on a critical examination of prevalent money myths and misconceptions that often shape financial perspectives. From the myth of instant financial success to the misconception that wealth equates to ultimate happiness, individuals are prompted to question these assumptions.

Unpacking money myths is not merely an exercise in skepticism; it's an act of liberation. By challenging these misconceptions, readers free themselves from limiting beliefs that may hinder financial empowerment. This process opens up mental space for a more realistic and resilient mindset—one that embraces abundance, acknowledges setbacks as opportunities for growth, and views financial literacy as an accessible skill for all.

Through this exploration, individuals not only shed light on the fallacies that may be influencing their financial decisions but also cultivate a mindset that is receptive to diverse possibilities in personal finance. Unpacking money myths becomes a catalyst for transformative thinking, fostering a mental environment conducive to financial well-being and long-term success.

Chapter 3

Building a Positive Money Mindset

Embarking on the journey of building a positive money mindset is a transformative endeavor that goes beyond traditional financial advice. It involves a holistic approach, integrating emotional intelligence, mindset shifts, and practical strategies. In this section, we explore key components that contribute to cultivating a positive relationship with money.

3.1 Cultivating a Healthy Relationship with Money

Building a positive money mindset begins with cultivating a healthy relationship with money. This involves acknowledging the emotional aspects of financial decisions and understanding that money is a tool that can be aligned with personal values. Readers are encouraged to explore their attitudes towards money, recognize any emotional triggers, and foster a mindset where financial choices become a source of empowerment rather than stress. Cultivating financial wellness encompasses budgeting, saving, and investing, but it also extends to finding contentment and satisfaction in one's financial journey.

3.2 Overcoming Limiting Beliefs

Limiting beliefs can act as roadblocks on the path to a positive money mindset. In this section, we delve into the process of identifying and overcoming these ingrained beliefs that may be hindering financial progress. Whether rooted in childhood experiences, societal influences, or self-perceptions, readers are guided through a reflective process to challenge and reshape limiting beliefs. By addressing these barriers, individuals can open the door to new possibilities and embrace a mindset grounded in abundance, growth, and financial empowerment.

3.3 Strategies for Shifting to a Positive Money Mindset

Shifting to a positive money mindset requires practical strategies that individuals can incorporate into their daily lives. This section offers actionable steps to facilitate this transformation. From setting realistic and empowering financial goals to practicing gratitude and mindfulness, readers are provided with tools to foster a positive mindset. Strategies for overcoming setbacks, learning from financial experiences, and staying adaptable in the face of change are also explored. By integrating these strategies, individuals can proactively shape their mindset, making informed financial decisions that align with their values and aspirations.

Chapter 4

The Psychology of Wealth

Delving into the psychology of wealth is a captivating exploration of the mindset, habits, and traits that characterize financially successful individuals. This section unravels the intricate interplay between psychology and prosperity, offering insights into the minds of those who have achieved financial success.

4.1 Exploring the Mind of the Wealthy

Embarking on an insightful journey, this subsection invites readers to explore the intricate workings of the minds of the wealthy. It goes beyond mere financial strategies, delving into the thought patterns, attitudes, and decision-making processes that distinguish individuals who have attained financial success. By understanding the mindset of the wealthy, readers gain valuable perspectives that can inform their own financial journey.

The exploration includes an examination of the relationship between risk-taking, innovation, and wealth creation. It prompts readers to consider how embracing calculated risks and fostering a mindset of innovation can contribute to financial growth. Ultimately, this section serves as a window into the mental landscape of those who have navigated the path to wealth.

4.2 Habits and Traits of Financially Successful Individuals

Success leaves clues, and in this part, we dissect the habits and traits that typify financially successful individuals. From disciplined budgeting to

strategic investment,
readers are guided through
the practices that contribute
to sustainable financial
success. This subsection
emphasizes the importance
of cultivating habits that
align with long-term goals,
illustrating that small,
consistent actions can yield
substantial results over
time.
Traits such as resilience,
adaptability, and a
commitment to lifelong
learning are explored as
integral components of the
wealth-building journey.
By adopting and
embodying these traits,
individuals can fortify their
financial foundation and
navigate the inevitable
challenges on the road to
prosperity. This
exploration serves as a
blueprint for readers to

integrate successful habits and traits into their own financial endeavors.

4.3 Adopting a Wealth-Building Mindset

The journey towards wealth is not solely about monetary accumulation; it involves adopting a wealth-building mindset. This subsection delves into the principles and perspectives that underpin a mindset conducive to building and preserving wealth. Readers are encouraged to transcend short-term thinking and embrace a holistic approach to financial decision-making. Cultivating a wealth-building mindset involves understanding the interconnectedness of financial choices with broader life goals. It encompasses strategic planning, delayed gratification, and a focus on creating value. By internalizing these principles, individuals can transform their approach to money, viewing it not as a mere medium of exchange but as a tool for creating lasting prosperity. This section serves as a guide for readers to cultivate a mindset that lays the foundation for sustainable wealth creation.

Chapter 5

Practical Financial Strategies

In the pursuit of financial well-being, practical strategies serve as the compass, guiding individuals through the complexities of managing money, making informed investment decisions, and navigating challenges with resilience. This section offers a practical toolkit for readers to fortify their financial foundations.

5.1 Budgeting and Financial Planning

Budgeting and financial planning are the cornerstones of a robust financial strategy. This subsection provides a

comprehensive guide to
creating and maintaining
an effective budget.
Readers learn the art of
allocating income, tracking
expenses, and setting
realistic financial goals.
Practical tips for creating
emergency funds and
developing long-term
financial plans empower
individuals to proactively
manage their finances. By
mastering budgeting and
financial planning, readers
gain control over their
money, fostering a sense of
financial security and the
ability to work towards
their aspirations.

5.2 Investing with the Right Mindset

Investing is not just about
numbers; it's about

adopting the right mindset. This section navigates readers through the principles of strategic investing, emphasizing the importance of informed decision-making. From understanding risk tolerance to embracing a long-term perspective, readers acquire the mindset needed to navigate the dynamic world of investments. Practical insights into diversification, research, and goal-aligned investment strategies empower individuals to make choices that align with their financial aspirations.

5.3 Navigating Challenges and Overcoming Setbacks

Financial challenges are inevitable, but their impact can be mitigated with resilience and strategic planning. In this subsection, readers learn practical strategies to navigate unexpected setbacks, whether they be job loss, market downturns, or unforeseen expenses. Insights into building financial resilience, adjusting financial plans, and seeking professional guidance equip individuals to weather storms and emerge stronger on the other side. By embracing setbacks as opportunities for growth, readers can transform challenges into

stepping stones towards
financial success.

Chapter 6

The Role of Mindset in

Career and Business

Understanding the
profound impact of
mindset on career and
business endeavors is a key
aspect of achieving success
and financial fulfillment.
This section explores how
mindset shapes
entrepreneurial ventures,
corporate climbs, and
aligns career choices with
financial aspirations.

6.1 Entrepreneurship and a Prosperous Mindset

Embarking on the entrepreneurial journey requires more than just a business plan; it demands a prosperous mindset. In this subsection, readers delve into the entrepreneurial mindset, embracing risk-taking, innovation, and a resilient approach to challenges. From cultivating creativity to viewing failures as opportunities for growth, individuals are guided through the mental landscape that defines successful entrepreneurship. Practical insights and real-world examples provide inspiration and guidance for those looking to build their own businesses.

6.2 Climbing the Corporate Ladder with a Wealth Mindset

Ascending the corporate ladder is not solely about professional skills; it's about cultivating a wealth mindset. This part explores the principles that guide individuals to advance in their careers. Strategic networking, continuous skill development, and a focus on adding value are emphasized as integral components of climbing the corporate hierarchy. Readers gain practical strategies to align their professional growth with their financial goals, fostering a mindset that integrates career success with long-term financial prosperity.

6.3 Aligning Career Choices with Financial Goals

Choosing a career is a pivotal life decision that should align with financial aspirations. This subsection provides guidance on making career choices that contribute to financial well-being. Readers are encouraged to evaluate their skills, interests, and financial goals to ensure that their career paths are in harmony with their broader life objectives. By aligning professional choices with financial aspirations, individuals create a synergistic relationship between their careers and long-term financial success.

Chapter 7

Solution to Finance Breakthrough

Attaining a financial breakthrough requires a targeted and strategic approach. This section provides a roadmap for individuals seeking to overcome financial challenges, identify areas for improvement, and implement transformative approaches to achieve lasting financial success.

7.1 Identifying Areas for Financial Breakthrough

Understanding where change is needed is the first step towards financial breakthrough. This subsection guides readers through a process of self-assessment and financial analysis. Readers learn how to identify areas where improvements can lead to significant breakthroughs. Whether it's optimizing budgeting, increasing income streams, or addressing debt, individuals gain insights into pinpointing the specific areas that, when addressed strategically, can pave the way for financial transformation.

7.2 Strategies for Overcoming Financial Challenges

Financial challenges are not roadblocks but opportunities for growth. This part delves into practical strategies for overcoming various financial challenges. From managing debt to navigating economic downturns, readers gain actionable insights to navigate challenges with resilience and creativity. Practical tips, resources, and real-life examples provide a comprehensive toolkit for individuals facing financial hurdles, empowering them to turn challenges into stepping stones towards financial success.

7.3 Transformative Approaches to Achieve Financial Breakthrough

Achieving a financial breakthrough often requires a shift in mindset and approach. In this subsection, readers explore transformative approaches that go beyond traditional financial advice. From adopting a growth mindset to leveraging technology for financial management, individuals are guided through innovative strategies that can lead to a paradigm shift in their financial well-being. By embracing transformative approaches, readers can not only address immediate financial challenges but also lay the foundation for sustained financial success.

Chapter 8

Navigating Economic Changes

The economic landscape is dynamic, and individuals need resilient strategies to navigate shifts successfully. This section provides insights and practical approaches to adapt, thrive, and transform challenges into opportunities during times of economic change.

8.1 Adapting to Economic Shifts

Adaptability is the key to navigating economic shifts. This subsection guides readers through

understanding and
responding to changes in
the economic environment.
Whether it's a market
downturn, inflation, or
changes in industry trends,
individuals learn to adapt
their financial plans,
investments, and career
strategies. Practical tips on
diversification, skill
development, and staying
informed empower
individuals to navigate
economic shifts with
agility and strategic
foresight.

8.2 Thriving in Times of Financial Uncertainty

Thriving amidst
uncertainty requires a
combination of resilience
and proactive planning. In
this part, readers explore

strategies to not only survive but thrive during times of financial uncertainty. From building robust emergency funds to strategic career planning, individuals gain actionable insights to strengthen their financial positions. This section emphasizes the importance of financial literacy and informed decision-making as essential tools for thriving in unpredictable economic conditions.

8.3 Turning Challenges into Opportunities

Economic challenges can be transformative if approached with the right mindset. This subsection encourages readers to view challenges as opportunities

for growth and innovation.
Whether facing job loss,
market volatility, or other
economic setbacks,
individuals learn to
leverage their skills,
creativity, and adaptability
to turn challenges into
opportunities. Practical
examples and success
stories inspire readers to
embrace change as a
catalyst for personal and
financial development.

Chapter 9

Teaching the Money Mindset

Passing on a positive
money mindset is a
powerful legacy. This
section explores strategies
for instilling financial

values in children, the importance of financial education, and how individuals can create a lasting legacy of financial empowerment.

9.1 Instilling Positive Financial Values in Children

The foundation of a positive money mindset starts early. This subsection guides readers through the process of instilling positive financial values in children. From teaching the importance of saving to cultivating a healthy relationship with money, individuals gain insights into nurturing a mindset of financial responsibility in the younger generation.

Practical tips, age-appropriate lessons, and real-life examples empower individuals to impart valuable financial values that will serve as a lifelong foundation for children.

9.2 The Importance of Financial Education

Financial education is a cornerstone of empowerment. In this part, readers explore the significance of ongoing financial education for individuals of all ages. Whether it's understanding the basics of budgeting, navigating the complexities of investments, or staying informed about economic changes, financial education equips individuals with the knowledge and skills needed to make informed financial decisions. This section provides resources, strategies, and recommendations for pursuing continuous financial education, fostering a culture of lifelong learning.

9.3 Creating a Legacy of Financial Empowerment

Building a legacy involves not just personal success but empowering future generations. This subsection delves into creating a legacy of financial empowerment. Readers learn how to pass on financial values, provide guidance to heirs, and contribute to charitable causes. By aligning personal financial goals with a broader legacy of empowerment, individuals can create a lasting impact on their families and communities. Practical steps and considerations for estate planning and philanthropy are explored, encouraging readers to think beyond individual success.

Chapter 10

11 Key tips to create a positive money mindset.

So, here are a few tips to help you improve your money mindset as you go along on your journey to building real wealth.

Remember, no matter what your current financial situation is you can change your mindset and money habits to achieve success.

1. Decide to be financially successful

Getting wealthy actually starts way before you open that investment account or make that first deposit into your savings account. It starts with a simple decision, which in itself is a very profound one.
It's deciding that you are going to be wealthy and that in turn means deciding to commit to the journey and trust the process. Deciding you are going to be wealthy (with full conviction) is an incredible boost to your mindset. This is because, with this

decision, you are telling yourself you can do it. Unless you believe you can be wealthy, you probably won't be inclined to do what it takes to actually build wealth.

2. Determine your life values

Once you've decided you are going to be wealthy, you have to determine your reason for wanting this financial success. That means determining your 'why". Your "why" drives a deep sense of purpose and helps you develop the motivation you need.
In fact, having a "why" can directly improve factors in your life that tie into overall happiness.
So why do you want to pay off your debt, save money,

become financially fit and successful, financially independent, etc?
Knowing your "why" will be your ultimate motivator. Especially on the days or during the seasons when things are not going exactly as you planned.

3. Let go of standards and focus on what really matters to you

When it comes to building wealth and working on your money mindset you have to go with what works for you and it's important to not get caught up in standards that are defined by the world. And you also want to avoid comparison with others; it's the thief of joy.

Again this goes back to your "why."

You might want to retire young, having $500,000 might be your definition of financial independence or perhaps it's $1 million. Or your financial goal might just be to have enough money to backpack around the world.

Whatever your goals might be, focus on your own standards and what money means to you in relation to what you want in your life.

4. Get comfortable with your fears and your discomfort

Anxiety and fear are natural byproducts when you want to accomplish something big. There's the fear of the unknown, the fear of change, the fear of failure.

And in many instances, fear can stop you dead in your tracks and can become really overwhelming. Especially when you start making up things in your head about all the "what ifs" and "whatnots" around what could happen (that more often than not, never happens).

The thing about fear though is that since it comes with the territory you really have two choices. The first choice is to let it keep you stuck. The second and better choice is to embrace fear as part of the journey, let it come along for the ride but let it know it's not allowed to hold you back.

One great way to overcome fear is to remember your "why" and look back at all the accomplishments you've had to date and the fears you overcame to get there. If you could get past those fears you can most definitely get past your current fears about money. For every fear you have, there is probably one action (even if it's just a small one) you can take to counter the fear. For example, are you afraid you'll never get out of debt? You can focus on making a debt payment right now or in the near future to work against that fear.

Remind yourself constantly, no matter how terrifying it can be, that you can do this and focus on taking small steps every day before you know it, you will have made big progress.

5. Express gratitude

Expressing gratitude is one of the best money mindset exercises because it is a good way to adjust what you focus on. When you are grateful, you focus more on the things you have that you are appreciative of as well as on all the good that has come to you.
Gratitude also drives contentment in your life which is key to wealth building because when you are content with what you have, you are less compelled to spend, spend, spend, in order to gain material satisfaction which doesn't always work

because you'll find that there's always something new that you can buy. Check out our 30-day gratitude challenge to get started!

6. Use affirmations to improve your money mindset.

It's so easy to let negativity creep into our mindset. However, you can combat those bad thoughts with good ones! Using positive financial affirmations as part of your daily routine is another one of the top money mindset exercises to start.
In fact, studies show that practicing positive affirmations can actually reprogram your brain! So, using affirmations will

improve your outlook and give you a healthy money mindset.

Check out our article on "55 Financial Affirmations You Should Tell Yourself" to stop the negative self-talk and incorporate more positivity into your thoughts!

7. Don't dwell on your past financial mistakes.

If you beat yourself up for your past financial mistakes, it's time to stop. Why? Because failure is the path to success! We all make mistakes and have had money problems, but you can use them to learn lessons and grow as a person. This includes bettering yourself financially.

So rather than dwelling on what you did wrong, use those past experiences as a learning tool to make a financial plan to do better.

8. Let go of limiting money beliefs.

Letting go of limiting beliefs is another key step to creating a positive money mindset. Limiting beliefs do just that...they limit you. You can achieve financial success if you try! So write down some big hairy audacious goals and set your sights high.
This is also another reason to use your daily affirmations. They will help you bust through those old beliefs and set new unlimited ones!

9. Get help with money mindset coaching and courses.

So, what's the best way to improve your mindset about money? Get help with money mindset coaching! The best thing is, it doesn't have to cost you a dime.
Clever Girl Finance offers free money mindset coaching calls with our mentors! Plus, we have over 50 hours of prior replay videos on a wide variety of money topics. We also have over 30 financial courses and worksheets that are completely free! Our "Build a solid foundation" bundle includes a "how to transform your money mindset course" so you can

go from a scarcity mindset to an abundance mindset. We also have completely free courses on everything from budgeting to investing, so you have the tools you need to become financially successful!

10. Follow fin-influencers to improve your money mindset.

Getting inspired by finn-influencers is one of the best ways to boost your financial mindset. They help you realize that they too have made money mistakes so you don't need to carry guilt or shame around for your past mistakes.
Listening to personal finance podcasts, reading books, blogs, and watching

YouTube channels will give you the motivation to transform your bad money mindset into a good one! You will also learn how to change your behavior with money, with tips on how to save, budget, and invest for your financial future.

11. Use money mindset quotes to inspire you.

Like affirmations, money mindset quotes can have a positive effect on your mentality. Reading quotes also have a "coaching effect."
They motivate and inspire you. So, using money mindset quotes can really help you when it comes to your financial mindset.
Here are a few of our favorite quotes to get you started:

"If broke people are making fun of your financial plan, you are on the right track." – **Unknown**

"You don't have to see the whole staircase, just take the first step." – Martin Luther King, Jr.

"The slightest adjustments to your daily routines can dramatically alter the outcomes in your life." – Darren Hardy

"It is not necessary to do extraordinary things to get extraordinary results." – Warren Buffett

"Stop being the chess piece, and start being the chess player. It's time to master the game of money once and for all." – Tony Robbins

Conclusion

The journey through "The Mindset of Money: Unlocking the Money Mystery for Financial Achievement" has been a voyage into the profound connections between mindset, personal finance, and the pursuit of lasting financial success. As we draw the curtains on this exploration, let's reflect on the key concepts, the call to action for financial success, and the invitation to embrace a lifelong journey of financial growth.

Recap of Key Concepts

Our journey began by unraveling the layers of

money mindset—
recognizing the impact of
beliefs, navigating the
intricacies of behavioral
economics, and dispelling
myths that often shape our
financial narratives. We
delved into practical
financial strategies,
understanding the
psychology of wealth, and
learning how to navigate
economic changes with
resilience and adaptability.
The significance of
instilling positive money
mindsets in children and
the importance of
continuous financial
education illuminated our
path, paving the way for a
comprehensive
understanding of the
intricate dance between
mindset and financial well-
being.

Taking Action for Financial Success

Knowledge alone is transformative only when translated into action. The call to action resonates as we urge readers to implement the principles explored—crafting effective budgets, making informed investment decisions, and embracing adaptability in the face of economic shifts. The transformative power lies not just in understanding but in actively shaping financial destinies through intentional, informed choices.

Embracing a Lifelong Journey of Financial Growth

As we conclude, we invite you to view personal finance not as a destination but as a perpetual journey of growth. The conclusion is not the end; it's a transition to a mindset of continuous learning, adaptation, and intentional financial growth. The principles shared in this book serve as beacons, guiding you through the dynamic landscape of personal finance.

In your hands, you hold not just a book but a toolkit for financial empowerment. The journey towards financial success is yours to navigate, with each decision, each step, contributing to the tapestry of your financial well-being. Embrace the journey, stay curious, and remember that every intentional choice is a brushstroke in the masterpiece of your financial success.

May your mindset be your compass, your actions be purposeful, and your financial journey be one of fulfillment and prosperity. Here's to unlocking the money mystery and embracing a future of financial achievement. The path is yours to forge, and the possibilities are boundless. Safe travels on your journey through the mindset of money.